M000301992

THIS
TIME
WE
ARE
BOTH

This Time We Are Both
Copyright © 2010 by Clark Coolidge
ISBN 978-1-933254-62-3

First Edition 2010
Printed in the USA

Coolidge, Clark, 1939-
This time we are both / Clark Coolidge. — 1st ed.
    p. cm.
Poems.
ISBN 978-1-933254-62-3 (pbk. : alk. paper)
I. Title.
PS3553.O57T47 2010
811'.54—dc22

       2010031701

Distributed to the trade by
Small Press Distribution
1341 Seventh Street
Berkeley, CA 94710
www.spdbooks.org

Available directly from Ugly Duckling Presse
and through our partner bookstores.

Ugly Duckling Presse
232 Third Street, E-002
Brooklyn, NY 11215
www.uglyducklingpresse.org

This book is made possible in part by
the National Endowment for the Arts.

NATIONAL
ENDOWMENT
FOR THE ARTS

THIS
TIME
WE
ARE
BOTH

Clark Coolidge

Ugly Duckling Presse 2010

A result of my first visit to the Soviet Union, *This Time We Are Both* follows the itinerary of the Rova Saxophone Quartet tour of November 1989: Leningrad, Vilnius, Riga, Tallinn, Tartu, and Moscow. The title is borrowed from a painting by Ostap Dragomoschenko. A CD of Rova music from the tour, also titled *This Time We Are Both*, was released in 1991 by New Albion Records.

—Clark Coolidge

for Lyn
for Arkadii
for what follows

When do images start to tremble?

— Chris Marker, *A Grin Without a Cat*

The beetle, beautiful as the shaking of the hands
in alcoholism, disappeared into the horizon.

— Lautréamont, *Maldoror*

Over near somewhere else there is the problem
of the difficulty.

— John Ashbery, "The Preludes"

I.

Dark hands pass
dark with no silence
lights in the smoke
hands that start, that light
pass the particles, link penetrations
to an amphitheater smell, that each corner well
treat the carriers, they small, they dark in the wind
the mind rose, the cable hands, a drench
of light smalls, close, a building of hair entire
how it dips in the time to see, we hear
they go forwards past
the inclination
darkening corners to form

The never rest dark forms a sample
a shattered sugar
blades in the dark near time
tastes more than dark but lines
then not to rest

Dark fur past
taste high window
elbow in move, placed than dark
height then links, pin strikes
wrist across, of pain takes a sample
septic smell of nerve say
but high, dare I light?

There is number, and it is a vanished vast here
broken cable of light sugar to pin on blue
flash particulars waiting, high down, tapped across
I live dark in particular waiting, city high and
over is the choice on this corner tonight

Time is in labels peeling, keep up the time-green neons
and spell a spark but past links air things swept
strike title the ways strong of pack smoke
gap to all this razor its windows
left of trap so I am one, my own but of two
over dicey caliper sweep, out of the well walls
one word dips to drop at a glance or
what if you lived over that streetlight change?
a certain soup, quick lead snap, snuff up
is the story of that corner
a lick snap spark to cross its rails
so dark the hands to cross with

Are you the one who moved, or me that came?
over these wells lived walls, a razor for windows
no neons for windows, in face the frames and blare wreck
today to dismal the fall repeats, unparticular labels titling out
peel from my spares, like nerve never rest never touch
now, what if soup in the streetlight change
straight to lick that rail then cross the palm
with steel as the sapphire fired its points
this seriously put together with tears, what is torn
remind, some signs replaced

But the neighborhood where the people, smoke
where the pole wires, a fist of needles and says
we extend farther than you do and will get you

no doubt of those poles wires in a fist
and I have the urge to shake you
flats of sun fill blind vitamins simply
share the urge to seize stars violet like soup from
that rail, pretend flat out those vistas are alarming
trolley pack, and spring, flash bait, wait and we wave
broken gum, a flat rock of sugar

A brown dawn wins with wireless opticals, rooves from which
the nerves retreat, and the standing so early is not to
release this corner
a shoulder full of hands, stop me if you've heard
but are these lights the same night? of turpentine wind
gnarls, full sail, grant dark its plain airs
the petrified bags, the polished TV
all in here above is not near
we are out, all night plummet, held around the same
a corner where these people show, regain a spot to urge
store down late to notice to stay, dark has its corners
where the same picks are made, tucks, grain spill
of the nightly spice truck, whatever will stay
denizen alert
belts all to their steel urge my plan

And gone off strung horn of coffees this horizon
motion?
at the darkness hurdles the people sleep on showing
off all dreams
to come from a time the coal in cones

II.

People from cities
laugh?
one calcium strip of the moon
people from talk
write?
cities lash us to their dawn writings
relax vitamins, release the shield
let it be blown out of all start
slant
so he open a sandwich before the fronts
wheel his bundles, makes
this corner of steel, alone of nickel
beckons a nineteenth-century lift of this place so flat
one night say for a start dunk your juice
fell through the darker juices, comes reoriginal with orebed
sign in limitless demeanor to tie it, be where
the people begin, wall beneath pyrite switch beside
sapphire points, begin what
to comfort the claims of steel, concrete?
I don't know yet
I belong to the rose of it here, closing too no limit
besides the again limit

Horse clops should come with these trolley joint torques
a viable leaning in the morning tin is to wait by it, not for it
jump across tunnels in the darkening air, the steel of a sort of
clam it seems, I look under arm to catch what swings
not these concrete ones, nothing alarming to a morning following
lights as they were, reminders, stores

Moon clotting through morning Leningrad bunches then there
what will we see?
sorts of moving how much further have I lived than this?
toward which we slow to see, book slant to start as at slate
engines at the wheat gate

Did cop to having what? lozenge orange trolleys right out
yellow of headlamps show a grammar line to rid lemon
sodas of an anciency
won't take more juice than an average holiday?
pass from substance to school, and back along its airs, nobody waits
at the flat rock of syntax
huge factory knock light lines all stub night long
and trouble to smear all the oil that swells, abatement
crosshatch in memory with sums of all railings by jewels
but only have I come to the marble gates
everyone stop at these walls

Are there resemblances? a smoking of the bread internalizes
chocolate from the hidden sea, not so sweet or so vanished in arc light
face up, factory Leningrad broad as the hawks do string
and wave drop and fill as in care, the lights turn up as faucets watch
increasing fields, there are more laps than you would expect
wash of sea caps
walking in the trolley beds and now the chocolate form the tower
from the lead-betraying time of the china font and low dead curls
wrapped itself in carelessness vegetable, a plane table on every hand
the lip to make the face over that we crest at the marble edge
a sort of plate to lay the note, to sound Italianate for the grey days
their ochres bartered for trespass, north of the kickball line to ride
a thought to wait on elevator of a number to do press forward
not a hate of heights floor the drop, a sky all water as we wake
a number without number, recoil your donut or missing keyboard member
a pillar kept in steams by the sea will not hinder

Then the streams open and Mordecai aches
he manages this klaxon of the poem
in fires
but balloons are spasms in this mental sort of wash
dye them
let it go be a city and night be one
of its vitamins in time a permission

Green stones the mind wraps its skin in this haunt, you
hand into the green storms, arbutus, tall length
been on the stage, I have slept sometimes, but
he lands there we are here, the tendency to haunt
the cases of last hard habit, tongued rather tailed
dawning not have we been dense for this, tunnel hued in
brighter than and kinder sorts collision smoke, facts have you
got in hats and then it smithers, help us on with, we are
the night loose to be carried by, and then by, can't it be
green linoleum light of a sulfurous, the great shell comet
a rising beet to be handing it on, as how when we were
and large shows up at the seats

They all twist past the food elms, this is indoors, which page?
we are trapped because of bridges their nature
sometimes is to be, some of the time is paint green
as for the smoke to rise, they are striped piano past
and it is a seldom quiet all down the space of real room
on our quiet knees and hands, no one else moves though they yell at times
so it adds, but an argument for which the adding? spells
pasts of the latest light, have you those locking pardons?
the master a couple of times the itch in smoke do you face beyond?
a whim time face pending whole beyond dips the damask, full rights
of display to depend, is he over? will the bridges and when
exactly rise? I see those bridges and I lock them

Which way and in a sort of red coat smell, wider?
position as well we learn in clothing, its partings to loan
and when the opening is over stride, dip it well, tell the model
dust to wait, I will furl and show, the clock will date
green there with lots of candy boots it, saddled with
hard habits, no place to, or bright stab someplace, for it to
is a substance on the average and in a position showing of all then coats
their tacks, I didn't think it needed, all those gnomes
underground wiring their lessons, jokes, marble wristlet into
weapon, pounds to the one bed, horns in flames, the rest
a helmet lesson, traded and scald in neat
make of one more of those doors for us held
bound without the light to

So we look at them how are you
a chemist the way you cheer? nearing a table with
all these plastic mimeograph sausage acts with the tilt liquid
bin in arches derrick on stage, plaid gangs to service them
and in noticing display articulate as you are in shoes, curdle sky
over all, we hear their wrists in theremin, thought attack
casts back the carrier, we are in thrall to the bags to bring pears
we walk past these bridges the same it was leather at that
laugh at the edges, where they trust, where you know yourself out
to a light so off it was bleeding cellophane, the limit
but then beyond that a standup take for increasing lessons

Do we in fact have nowhere? it is us in the lines
they talk to each other in stages, they take and in fact have
a rate brown wooden for their mention then notice someone is missing
where we have been, some, particle in the side room to the launch
is spoken in jungles as particular physics, or count your weapons
crullers, they nod then bow and deploy a sort of showup pinhole
so sort of it's slow and in serried harms
this listing of the smokes, the man in the shirt

This whole in its riverside vows is a history of shoes
the man on the bench, the one in the smile, the one in the back of
the buckled slats, painted out and trembling for snow and what follows
only five walls left, nobody totaled it for, in voice
or in keptness, magnificent when loaned out full
of image voice in hand toward this poster in ken, cough
if you wish but there are only pictures of trees, folders giving
tendency to juice in them, pen on the knees, drains in the tents
cold and want in palm glass scope in sole declension
steel points to sapphire, so marked naked avenue, tiring of less
but few are truly the few

But we are not still though they are, brass at the concert of shouts
dash, dash, try back in, neighbor
the light in the jungle of heights, a heat of nails a unison
the least of them all in a dull olive dive, shaken not paginated
black signed as closed wheat at rates we enter the door another
chlorinated to the spines of it all away from us too, high G
at the prongs, bed to the knees, for us you, for you the tugboat
does spend more twines than it snarls, gone harder at it
too to add, as if acted does spend, and wider as do none
but the syncope, passage back to the lacy heart
we go, attic of the ruby boule, there is heat then there is no heat

Bring us this back better together and you bring it lighter
touch for a luck your vitamin not so often the hill where we go
we light and the vine at this stage and some knees to apron
of a thought, will it ever start again? this hill of the only
light thoughts, nailed unisons, he leaps then another kicks his heels
we are losing him out to sapphires in the stages as ladders willing
of whisper light, dramaturgical light of the big pickle he lost
the mate to by all he has ever stored heavy by or rattled to
a calypso, she sleeps by, enter she in this room of the song to

the sky of barely beneath, and all of us here, some pipes in there
strike liquid to fire and green where it isn't, or even what
blown up into a sprain period are we left with? dots
sperm bank on glass shelves iterate, trombone of a fig
grow near, spell by, a normal hand up in leathers of these woods
interior and with gold smells and gems quite late, his name
here was Snow, become too light to ever wholly clear
we all write it down by a drop of the pipe

Same as this clear you were, so nothing found based on out
the titled door on a hug, a sneeze, the bearing of January
in gold hinges, we don't have, less than the night for
grown into things, these turret tapes and kennel singings
he was voted on for lobster twilight of a violet then sat
them there and the beer at a low table or two talked
it was invading chat, so is he then tapping
touching greens so even the browns seem, friday the night we all
and other capers of the bent, out into one huge vent build
colossal fuel haul display, all that and our neighbors their
part trends and clasp habits, brute stem in winter mild, tastes
light at the clip of any stable wall and we'll have it collect
and dull and this after all done from what in a second
pressed into endless pairs we have borne it, this
aisle of blown bone

III.

Then who has fallen in with the sound?
axis of question living here or having the light to
fall on Eventualstein, the country of manyskin
locks have been taken of all this morning lingo
rakes in a far window or the helm of this
smog of stacks that give little calm for
treat avenue, imbroglio lesson, why has, which hatch
a head of ideas that are driving me, attached face
redline kaput time-length Aurora, kept up with
filled in quick, leave the leash and watch these icicles
where mole has a magnetic foreskin, says

Walking the wetness dry
about out of head
trim concrete to the trees
stay lovely

Broad avenue sweeps? we took them
Nevsky Prospekt, a microphone extension and ladder to nowhere
then Henri Rousseau with popcorn in his arms sights the time of day
by a redface watch, nothing to do but have nothing to want
them watch everything, put a sundown shine on the revolution,
rose is its name, have a velocipede out of it

Then has a try through all these primes to the stone
or plate beneath known as witness intake
a bareness to nevertheless dark, and in tune with strain
we woke in here on a beam of smoke, looking free
down on the alarming baking lane and sod, may part
to the opening of time, unavailable ledge or
plain tree the siren under which

Any of this, beneath whatever lack of sun or hunch, reads?
a window, such as hold that next attempt and bracketed
by roof-edge pipe to drain at the foot, I hear you
will all this haul back on us? mostly turning to
trust on this sphere now disc to thrive us an answer
is it or just past it on
a certain training level to try
this night and its silk-laced whatever wheels

I go by as ever on pencils
underneath of every leaving sun reveals
twigs in bottles in threes, elsewise an etching erasing
grease for the eyes, that they take away nothing
this alarm prospect from, team through its gates
this pin shine scrutiny whatever comes, or Aurora leaks
else most greys, andirons wild go creak at corners
something something else and us will live by

The rest? the further
inside corndogs on limegreen street parts
could tell he said by it but not in time
it was not
invented but lived through until
where Eskimo Pies were invented, just
the name dodging on the sheet beyond bareness
in the winter well, I smile they don't
there are trees to turn to heat left, no?
a rattling bacon of fences wired, then rave
just spells recalled for pencilers, replacing doers
reconciled with their habits, clothing weights, nubs
of sense inverted the man at a crack has said
impossible to investigate dogs or underwear with watch on
so I duck, that I last, that they dodging smile
at the Abraham and Isaac in the Rembrandt basement play versions

one where the facehugger was born, was it ever?, dulcimer closing
we passed that basement, then corndog battery and any
slips to the front of the bus and on condition
gradual opening, Guadalupe, Guadalcanal, names
schist of an army blanket

Arrival at the Blessing, snap, candle in the wind
and borrowing apples, to foolscap those satisfiers
zoos may arrive from these cloth pencils, I live arrayed so
I live in heaven nearly above the bra factory, shortening works
quickly how the maze hard glass to advantage clamps, tucks
I couldn't keep from, budge I couldn't handle
all these paltry walks 'neath tunics of squid in window
such twigs in the salad, bereft, let's wait, which are the salad
something come to something on the brawn heights, what clots
will advance us? we must believe in no further
advantage but betterness, and yet still
in the house I can hear this smell
arrival at the mentioning shade

A balance perhaps a screw loose will
turn the corner inventive of horn
then to him him, close of day and sew the sky and clang
his dog and rightly stown advantages in old tile shack
is buried precise beneath City Central, knob of the revolution
certain smells, like dives but further out, crowd control but from
this stage of swarm event, no clots to those furrows
I'm happening, says the salvage man up the nights
he stays in there, down to core tantamount to Kelso
laid beneath the tiles of Komsomol Heaven
tune to no one's reaches click anymore
a Jain version of Ahmad Jamal

Loose, was he telling you advising you're better off
for a race through the ice and almost aloft carrying the
stations of what on your backs, and shown in the wind
those glances last evening lashed to the stage, of television
was it said, he conducted the stringer parts the heart leaps
on lemon tubs from there, given a sort of banana tone
are you guys what or what? bunch up, aim the jungles
save us some salmon smoke striped for the stairway
to a weapon stone build, so now
we're friends which one has the name?
in that's the rub of all time

Turn the tube, it's the Sound of Ragout Reveal
the all of more least, said Dominique my lead daughter
tending to store a constant mere landing, owl covering
tampered in testing the president's spar lunch, and in farm time
impression speciality but proud of another fork, further bulk
from calling which to selling of yourself a bit much
when summer's well and you're honking here, a trouble
Maria, for which this blender here in the cargo on matchtips
a gratefulness for peace she reaches the books out from under
finding you funny but off a bit of noise too left, can do it
though and buys it all in like a snare, more than on treble there
the TV's tea is a Morgan's tea, the more ease monk or even silly
dome marine, when all the world does its thinking, mysterious
crayon stream in which world prong, the eating club put out
by word metallic raised the point, if that was an author
doesn't obscenity, anacrusis, what? is as much of
an ace as I count an acid queen? inspect we the
garlic duller dream in which morality comes geodesic
present to you moray eel, gentlemen, hand me the duck
I need to come nick him, whose crochet was
of granite not vodka, this time generic

of all fools and not a car lay there or not, that's what
he did so, bought himself a weather

Collapsed and then the dome but called on insanity to wait
it's not furnace yet naturally, rolling on sundays though
put a fit on, a war dinger or modern wit steamer
instruction left off the more needed drug, a spacial pacifier
for which wars have been stroked and named, whatever way
the crested bronze gratuitous, or do we parade deceit?
but another gym novel took the brunt of Francisco Spheroid
not daring any one the frond scratcher of hideous dangler do
was it that Mr. Hemmings booted? is nicht
or one's book or bullet are in trouble, sleep then let
the blue sky dangle on you when you gotta stop meeting
jolt, heaven up, Buddha down
a coal canceling tryst of the now heavy sell, get that
number of subgum Vikings to settle up, and their numbers for
a pretty gushing good or mining afterbelly sat on
we gingerly
kiss on stealing your book a further wait they pushed me to
could not find a fin of the silence, rub of the alarm
in allures could not cock and titty you but be one such bastard guy
a blur under lamps, or Ruby Foo as a drunk of her time
by the elbows a pretty dull child, don't answer
could make the dock maroon of a distorted New York City
back for them, or bring select blueberry chip to the bra works
inner lorry of the buck artists in today's Sunday's movies too
I in effect fan my needs, sling them all betray
which it seems she'll need to plumb shot lime
deign the news for sniffed husks, those curl dusted bar lines
and don't forget this Dracula escapes from a mighty narrow desk

The unquestioned answer rose tonight too, through

the twins' mesh into furthers of a whole other two
an unexplored life in that territory hallway, the touch
is up in the lights, fell out it was
a firm as if broken waspish tapping into the night
the crystal exchange valences
sapphire stew of the willful out sign
and listen to them high with the apparent one
in organ belfry chatters, as if the brain
unloaded hours of drums, reed hoards of slants
aiming, admiring, sugaring the old salt
crystals exchanging valences
he said what he never dug he now digs
in previously unquestioned territory
at least the answer mesh rose

From anacrusis to plain, remove the cellophane
definitely nothing in Pythagorean deserts looking for Bantu sulfates
got to jettison hone or lacerate grin
pin in Billie's finger, jazz had gone home
was late anacrusis, a steady hour of night on a platter
stand in a doorway and we shut that night
by play of bumper doors obeisant to steer as half a car
or a leg up on beady feminism, anacrusis?
voices gelled from tube, are they metrical?
left the mind set on color, where are you?
as if pressed up the back, initially but then
it's a first, we are blessed on the weak beats

IV.

Wonder wheel, then again in neon
colors the predreams, they even took away the nightmares
potato pinnacles all vanilla and mattress tick whines
sappiness incarnate, taken to be sapphire in peridot
hold out solid for the days, the nights remand
the rest of the inlays, streets with no tags
lugging in the distance, as if tobacco conversation having

Sharpen off the edges, riding these streets, so much
apparel and given, the puncture of being, a skim, a notch
of a landed mend, half a hallway as could disappear in
then tappings on the lam and we do go, all's
a notched paraphernalia to a landing where
the water is wise, the words to steer

A man that's captured, what can they do
he's lasted as far as building things, granted
they're cogs in a ledge, but stream, I could count on
everyone being taken out back of the harms in the way
of a block conversation, all the way down those palaces
hallway transitives with their hive followers, even
iced lions with stares, regalia
note the pen inside, and anacrusis bent to it again
where, insure, an orange organ for retraining or
the ladder to nowhere laughs

You have to be quite willing to be dumb in the case
the lace doesn't quite cover an opening, the streets come within
we calm and burn, packets laid out in a cast utopian here
and in green raised to brown, a certain interior brown all vast

he was trained to keep the television on at an angle, in memory
all the sun you could ever hope to laugh in, chuckled to
a harvest tent, sprung remembrance a matter of bars extend
or tuned the stubs, checked his cast

Coat, by a length of optic gel, the pear
saw we couldn't drink enough to suit it, quite eyed and fast
apparent the last night an increasing bust to be lost out
quandary enough sounds are but a broad mica failure
recorded at a lope, reoriginal avenue, nowhere more eventful
and small

A bottled water called Eccentric Sky, remain
the bottle of water it says Electric Song, don't touch it
for echt take it easy tonight the 17th, is it right? for to laugh?
but just to play it all in grey fills, a snow peak beneath it
in nothing but that green got bumped then? in grey fills
it all off a notch toward heaven in steady plan, we hunch about
taking time is different than keeping it, the hands are drier
so everything's closer
to

Some of them then soon got the hang of the winning
a brigade in health colors, no storm no less, these hens
are weak under here, too flat, an alien body type
all limbs on the one side, laughter, then the grey falls
well, are you ready to paper the doorway? can of days

A man in a box rearranged
his original head
an owl's head stood out, next
a rod bearer of tidings not exactly mixed
framed, bent, originally over

a puff above, I write because
I was sent these
tires to the brim for cashdollars
got smart, came in, had to call you
up in trembling and little left the city
for all you

As found you
out to keep, hear in train
to wear what's tawny, wearing the maps
caught inside an amp's box, the crayons
at an angle, to puff on barely
and nowhere to phone you, listen
he has held us a day, or has he
given it? things such as diamonds
sound as well

In this sky a racket of diamonds, Rollins lighter fluid
the kelp here is made up from the basement on, nicotines
as much as white diamonds dry on the card
as the smoke ceiling puts out tones in pure hums
you could tell, my house was a hole
through to the Russian Territories where bodies
could mold themselves in an atmosphere of their own words
sigh and mold themselves to
my mouthpiece speaking, give me a handhold
that and a carrot juice
to fall over forward, gypsum, famous
and find yet a different route, a parrot
this time we are both

By the things that the man had brought to his cell
I learned that the grey and black birds are crows
there was a guy back there in a long coat

I saw them, turning, Russians
emerged in a throng, fronting through murk
ordinary avenue, night blank
time we were leaving, they were just there
for pencils and for period
black
peajacket and tongs the aurora stains

The effect of heads on the body politic
a certain slant of knowing how does Marshmallow go
so the sun came out on those tracks while we spun

V.

The train is
ink in half, the rest said
is background music
the yard, based on what goes by?
take the upper one, we'll roll anyway
drop to the foldout desk, two feet
at last is based on what? the train
often enough at rest or the other, appears he's scoring
a whole strip through tank country, aisles aflood
did you find there was ink in the past, creekside or frostside
banks for antenna spots, waits on hexagonal racks
borscht for breakfast with the unknown floaters, sinkers
spurn, bend to window one not wave, met to
consume, slat pass, slight cease, felt bells
in drama, Cheyenne station stone tower in a pause
all of the cement cast telephone poles
wonderful suggestion, burned past repeat
repeat repeat repeat
repeat

If I only had the one table
but the only problem the table
keeps moving in space

But I only note the bells when they pause
here in the Literal Lounge we speak space
not to score the living room linoleum of this tooth room
it's only made out of tin that you walk out cleanly into the day
only after the other decently harnessed adventurers, wish I could
play, wish I could write, the air rubs snapping

only then did we roll to the point of mist
and then did we list ourselves recently
past

This
is the only way I could find to get rid of it
the top came off the sky, then stuck
with a whole lot of space to avoid ourselves in
as grandfather's chimes announce the news, a blessing
we all but pass up, nod off trembly
rapt, at an equally trembly sky
the nerve we were in

Here it's the singers have all the magazines, the doctors are women
the snake that's missing one roll, north of true
the silvers make circles and the lower ones yellow
so here archaeology arrives at the mouth, a month
to calm down, we get there all too soon
so soon it's erased, you see the mouth go
it's studies, auctions, see it all get caught
in the teeth of the moving stone

Birch forests, firs
ash, handles, time
the train starts to waddle, we prove so
insufferable, that have no mechanics
to don the wheat in tandem, pause
to wrestle, stub the tube, I never knew
your poodle was questionable, slip up the handle
but always move out beneath the light

Allow the lengths coarser and coarser caught, brighter
then brighter left, the trunk going off at midnight, alas

octagonal dress and pants of cement
fancier constructions in these low hills
coming now to
gain a whiteness, but did I only from the back?
preempted by barrel roll, stocks to the side, grease mention lower
how much of this locker is high tension grinder
in-town job lot, enjoyed?
outside just now it sat quiet in rhyme

Elementary as an elasmosaur
barely there, but dear
has been entered here what? the people stand out in
the capital of not just another, repetitious wader of
cement walks and loud roads, battery eyes in case
an answer aimless double rubber baby bubble ramping, shaking
I know where they go, to death but that
these people don't have to refer to
space to feel on time, there's a hole
in the republic shaken by us, we have no more rope
so we take the train, your room is risen
the room where your train is now ready

People, in their heights
gain approach road status, exit poll by Eddie Bracken
peace, it escapes, curls out from under the space statue and gone
honk of geodes in a line lit on voltaic malnutrition
I get a log house here somebody else keeps the key

To the hummable dream of La Brea on the gabbro escalator
we know you have points here too
Vilnius in a room, tiny but no one switches

No authority, don't wipe the window
with the red and blue aerials, they dip and dally and
the man after awful is matched in snow
goes up, had never played with us before
naive La Brea on the Lake, he houses in the bay for the boats to clear
the one, this should a might be better than last night's
clear to the sky mild key to stay in

You've changed, the belter of your rage is gone
the cleanup comes before the song, Dexter lays the instruments
long grey coats drape streets to the palace of fine maps
now he's the pencil sailor, redecorated, about to solve
a pine on your manual, the country of much less

Plastic though, they have it, dousing like sperm head
the beads, we turn them, amounted out of it stayed
next to the drummer the only voice that's louder, well
said, impenetrable accompaniment anomaly, watch your vines
as three green stalks light hard on a fizz of zoo
so count to ten, broken laugh of myself now the tamer
where is our standby? and have you got out the lighter?
never such a glorious mixmatch as the overlaid wrong pattern
the eight-bar police won't allow you to see but can hear
there's never enough juice through that wall, or melody
of no Lenin, the string of doves up, the ladder lighted down
got the play just about glassed along those lines its own
lines, the struggle pulled

Wouldn't weave you a worsted of this sort of banditry
thought a scent of circuitry but for sample survival instead
a corner lot throttled up and headed by all comers
have the stars out on a length of that same rope
here we come to play the future

VI.

Parks
cars
in the dream of the farm on the day of the questions
an andiron laid on a sawhorse
a sapphire dropped on a firehouse
cars that come from far in their place
reminiscent manners which must be answered
as just other members of the trap, do you think
locked in the mode will hold you up?
then she answers, it's just what Alice plays
when she comes downtown, and I say
you think she should have stayed in Oz?

Reminiscent of cars that let us into churches
by the side he is cast in expression of Baltic lostness
how to come through in one smudge of the haste
of crystal wattages the world has lent its lenses
then walk you forth on beercake hide in one craven snap?
an ounce of luck has left its least leash attached
that he burned through to the back fabric of his habits
lined up some stairs of gabardine and shot them, a bargain, one to
lift with, though the voiceglass comes down behind the eyeholes
some losses that gain speed then the joke of it is
replacement manners back of all circuitry, stop me if you've heard
this dell in the wake of the way
use the glass one only on prepared twines

Buses and cars in hard repair, bare walls
rubbed the crayons from their sides, scream tones in
alarming tendencies, tobacco lines a Baltic legend

the Queen of Grass Stains, nature?
one was part of it but not close to it, when

Hole in the story, castle of the century, for the single word Trak
has them yell Empty Body to unknown sanctions, makes up itself
the original home of emptiness fills with blood, silence with fluid
blocks made of crustacean stone, that was the whole of it
the machine conversational and with ropes, are we up here?
to the point of crenulation the painter of phenol straws and
brothel postures buys a mainline for his auto, put it there
through cold home rooms housing horses of glacial origin
comes the plan for the original home, a lace of beads to fold snakes
get it on in emergence the fade to Emergency Lake
where it's cooled enough we climb stairs

Wash further around the new bricks so much faster the hotel begins to
shine
but it's a castle starts to show another language, one this time with
use it to exchange old gods for new money, ungawa!
ten may do the gods while thirteen punk out in the off slugging
or so do some the pry with me, the rest of the gods one
pricey jest or noble lump, an odd slug in prisoner zone
or stretch zoo, that gouache wick hand me for the hotel gap, yes and so
most of these Rehoboth type scenes just miss a lot of vastness

Apportionment
northward from the center of tune permission
an aisle of a lake, pencil in light, abrupt sends
link a solid ape of its stone to toe perimeter, in mesh sort
a pet and perfect pocked amber sewed to, I mean it
the angle it slights they don't show anymore
slight grey stopping of the ship to relate
its soldered dock or Ship of Hoy

permission of say your shirt to dip in one of the old bop bromides
saddled with the telling well and stoned here, zero of the cake
saw to the tolling around every

Terrains tonight rose
so was found space around every
time the globe integers whistle feeler meaning
no explanation but penetration in a natural
light attribute of that, one possible habitat
he found the right rope, and then nothing as a double bonus
tie his shoe and take the boat to nonexistence?
filled up with the scrapped miles of this trailer, how you would have us?
find the right sort to tell of say Great Whites, pictures of eyeglasses
or the holes behind them, I'd have to see fit to set some other
sailor out on a solo for one of you, of all the other fours of four others
this four fed it all perfectly, no one could tap a vitamin past it
the flown proof

So no more sketching
structures, which in
are sketched? but a day spent
in castles marks the time, a glass of all golds
the nine things before you
take the tenth, stop them
or hand them on, the scald you don't see can
make your veins steel, the perimeter I
alert had wiped the brake from fast
enpurpled to press out to a ballast of columns
the brace out front calms the hips, try to loosen
the train that parted and little left of
this grace stops silence in a wade of noons
could come invent the spodumene riff
oblongs to arrive, parked in a light

It's a terrific care we haul here in Siluria Broken
dropped just that crustacean, as the clock comes off the wall of glass
its cogs meet that we should hold the key
to a knock attack is a blanket with no maybe
gained to myself of a surer you I stare myself along
your grace to a folded stone
worked to a paddled storm
there is no natural habit

VII.

What time? that time you, and you
so some deep pig comes to tell me, buy
then vanish into a white of pajamas
fused, where the wrecking iron toilet doesn't work
whistles in the dark and makes its, given things
firm wall of the whole street over
trolley points, crowd whisper, cement standard
peace, upraised and among
the bullet-headed duck doesn't like me, is said
wants dissolve our silver compact
out from under and in trading, we're so high here
pieces of the invention of then the slave
deep imitation gone awry, cap used as clock
or at least its bill, points to the trading pieces
from up here on cement, I could but couldn't give it up
so Palookas of the ozone meet, trade baths, write facts
like Trinity Makepiece came and told me, you
can't open this, crack it, as big birds grey
give it up beyond glass, couldn't cap our ills
but toy with my tissues on which iron poems
rung the rites of freedom, or a complex
or at least the tone of its plants
the knuckle of their launch, its bench, cogged hammers resting
not a lot of illimitable oil solve but you trust me
I'll cable back the whole, shabby torn entry, he wants me
in the hallway goodbye, like an ample
hello, score for echo to agglomerate, that kind
the third time we are math, we are need

So must have it that
the art hang in dirt strips
a black sulfur liner nightmare at the lost steps
gold center permission steps, coiled it was supposed
gathered us later, nips off the primus bottle
he barrels his works, a lug in the weld dark, brute stains
handling down fraught and desperately occasional but doused prime
diamonds where the wood bends, in fact you can see, floating
all the tiny Olympics that were lost under here, thick
meanwhile and only with pickets
Ich bin so frei, with pockets
your hand works

Mine is in simpler baby bottle gold in ducal pairs
the celluloid to a lozenge heater, my contributor
over behind the pipe wall and vented bending bargain sketch
slatted and gutted cymbal leftover gleamy pasticherie
quick now, every foreign word you know, the longer
the better we are the word police, the sharper the public attachment
to structural umbilicals, wind within their hollow walls
the whatever construed to be hid within, spun on tenement control
time to march back as the dust blows
a Martian has landed on the human moon

Some kind of depths attack space, reduced to one
spare triangle, we pass its dusty handle at the river bench
where everyone turns at the celluloid wires, the map in case
the nobody more than knows, these squids of a love match
their battery makings, lost in a bevy to darn down the street
tapped light or with laurel won't retreat, be as me
on a lark, or listed as hitter on one desperate thrust to the counter
they are just a little loaner, now can this dark go so city
and it sticks to the walls, Approach Beers

played out to the creature they sell at every corner
these days that go past all the time

Streets, these that lose to dazedly open space?
made up however to someone else's measure, he tripped
the fan, arrayed his numbers in a mongrel belt, came off lazy
the boy that landed on banana moon against all edges?
where waiters, those loaned-out standers, those bounders
down basements to lounge, matriarchal lacewing of the cherries
I erect the facing fencing signs that all's corrected, even done
so critical of the drawbacks, fenders with handles, we'll strip it
scout it all for the corners where the snow makes other corners
it's possible to fly like a fish, what all else?
it's even to be a friend with measure, fade down avenues
that the song of the airplane glue singes, in here perforates panels
out there times our lunches, two bras to go until the clock
or are they only of the glass in stretches?

Mark it as adhesive final and cross the Neva
drop all your blocks and laugh, continue to roll
the policemen of their pretense, so threadbare it is
that I live at cross purpose to a point in Nevada
Stroller Domes it is
fires came out of the wall there and
art hit
the bolts out of the Neva in a final drop
the way you'd say it to have him hit it and
art stop

I'd like to be a fraud there
if I could wave a tray of truth then
the way it beckons it has not been answered
even the hallways that could level grade

this cotton bent of light, this socket to disgrace
of
the gynecological frenzies in their plastic cases
wedded to a clash, this sort of iron, in blonde crosses
attics full of harm bones at cleat rates, that elevation
a very entry tired of the eye
an even clustered cough of the toe
a pole on which you can chair or chain
those chopping permits given on dusted panes
it's alarming the tops to the same scale how many

Beneath this trestle the trained throats all catch
can you come without touching?
below the light below the ground
below any sort of basis
you were trained to think you could handle me

But he was, like as his limiter pierced, a costy owner
a sort of born practitioner, lemon olive suit of the louder drawers
getting the slant on the horn blew at that picture, you know
that tame mountain glary-eyed one, the slave with his own deck
heard of such permits as houses its sorts, which we'd all fall
together to try
a torch to the suit in armor he was then, so
humor him, Jacoby, scratch a horn of that stripe

Ghoster of all the giant ones he overlaps plans
half an apple through the roof reliever, denser
then fades so we eat in the dark
on top, a snap, the one
you've only to threaten by tall building
the iced rivets round the edge of nothing
in particular, available to chewing in the free height desk event

I made it past the edge of waiting, do you go
beyond the violet line, adjust your mouthpiece
get your head around the headpiece
they took us all around in neon the top of
nobody to know for sure in these zones
so hand me that cadmium black of the circular zoos

Have you had to take in these advantages of snow?
I did drill the mice some new high lines
now with the pocket reinstalled, the refrigerator rushed, or rested
watch in snooze reverse, it's nominal, this room or wedge
these streets a recall of schistose pendants
having to do a lot of farms, it's twilight
where he got them ripped, she tells us watch the skies

Meanwhile I'm yawning on a whole room of asbestos
Iron Farm where only in the collective sense do things get stretched
started, Fu Manchu At The Stake, a corrective ripper, or ripener of salts
call it, Never Mind
call it, Salary
call it, Brains Behind
call it, Salary
all masters of the carbon arts griefs

A pair of perfect sapphire night matches
iron rivets in a watch position
or the time transition, a false faint
a tone lower than your wheat socks is the tire tread
just wait up for my mouth to water I thought
whipping it belting by, high as a tree with wiseguy advantages
the full skull peep, a just rope of which we had not the awareness
will not ripen the date of away in the air
of a thinnest algebra, disappearing tin, rewinding rhyme

and in a cape yet, the Varlet Bastid has danced on
my causeway a double shovelful of bells

This route leads to the Palace of Doors
ages since the years we balanced those drains
what waits down that avenue the brain stores?
the socket watchers will circle your chamber

VIII.

The morning spent looking for Gogol's shoes
the dream trod seeking a substance to abuse
guess he wants me to see him, or viable lessons thereof
and down will come the cement mixer, or loosener withal
long will slide a tongue there all by itself
goosed in the avenue of oiled stones

Did he dream of waiting for the piano to arrive, come now
on living stone for an anteroom floor, that base, such a hook
there are watercourse carvings and slots for wooden nuts
we see by then he has come from a long way and is still not quite here
yet rely on the food he, video array and paper racks he
in fact a whole hall of drugstores, his piano is too wedged
and even we have not yet come

Did you put out any of the sown felt in a want meet for them to see?
I would throw in a sow for a rifle as well
feel like swapping your child? you're talking like one
it's time we left, you too? the rest of it all let them rot
what's more, that rifle is no common object, the way
a pig would turn out only one rank lower in this single world, the way
everything still is now

We go, so it's not here
we left much of an else to the road, going
up to this it goes off with us, shot of the bus
short one headlamp grained in the dust, it rings
and the road sides, turns come to throws in a mirror
one admonished further, put your food where your mouth is

I clapped, then the radiance
contrasted white breath to the ivory slab, loaves in heat
sent in a pinch between windows between highways
we want a way, we want the link to prod a window
the odd of invent it and thought such that massed
before us the regular lyric prong as basis and asymmetric at any moment
waves of wheat the way these streams of the way
widen to the odd of invent, cap the pen a mirror nearer so
not to stick on the crooked why not lace structures
sun cast on snow oiled from barns, massive the matches
stuck along route, of things he would begin to hang then on the outside
our invention of the lyric link becomes "I am an able dock"
so we bend from that again to stars in beads of the amber
left here with the ambers that cannot be cut
he drives faster so as not to leave water on the book

I cannot hear a recording of the oiled stones
reorder then fill, bake and adjust, idle in place, shuffle
all available charts in arrears, they so gear this grain
it goes white and leads us, the bug
sent off as a stove bolt hiked up to the starry
basis original overleaf standby, can you
come on duty without touching, slouching?

Miles till we go without wheat or light
on top of the jokes till we monkey finally
in an aisle with the very bases, turnarounds
their plotted ashes while on paper it purples
sing out these windows, all the dusts come stump in a line
or stooping to blind throats in a different light
those odd birds gorgeous that appear as pencils alone
above, see
and then she started a month of those mumps
see manual

Told there are hairs along this highway, getting filler
is it mapped? spot a biscuit areaway with its inked-in hoards
never could we think of selling so salivating going down bent
on the true though nights of it out by the horn haul lodge
no, really, a double pass of great tongue, all this
cement hurries the sun down

That supreme that obscures, or an unclear mask
and what's behind the sand in those trucks is celebratory
I have wanted none but minks might mate by meaning?
but no two antecedents ride the body the same way
make rights of way for them, more snow and fewer signs
that's in place of sky of blue the sure poetic ticket, last me
believe it, the red army should come short in Lithuanian time
coats on, shopping over, go home, what else?
it says here in red, it cuts here in slab
below zero on this window

A rival ambiance of cordiality, or to harrow
and fewer farmer cars but holes in the snow river float past
on dread reefs of the felt stare Bright Mississippi would go over well
here a snap there a bolt, where big molar in frozen field is
a historical marker, where the bands of wheat are the trees
where are and why think of
any midwest?
miles to go without weight or break
upon pencils alone, no hills

Five thousand feet and missed not a digit, landed by
Green Tractors, the name of the tune the Monk here would write
in his ovening bluecoat and bent or bending Lincoln
humming in his pace past gaps, instead
accumulations of trash held up in air by strings of height

44

it's all in a painting, otherwise it's a new cement that never quite
reaches crystal state, a lump of the gatherings in its way, but
all that rose bright once lost is left for sad
load of snow cemetery for its close crosses

So what's the mad once boy now man to do?
rust it out of a bucket into soda biscuits?
much raw lust is lost in the process, lost flesh process
and in upheaval, big cakes drawing down the River Canteen
we'll flail for it, a mile till they hold up my Buick, readier than
that green that only shines in windows, trouble green, what
I was born about, that battery acid Dentine stew
more than the other people there a balancer, and happy to
get me a big green bird made of wood and let me set it, just
these people were prisoners of their own followers
and boy, the mice

Snow goes on the overblown way, lied to, struck
and stored away, we have reasons, the planet
of hinges buried to its edges, sledge bearing salamander
could repeat off into micro farms, with boards and pocks
nothing to do with, did you eat or fish? darning
needles of a temper, glassine glove covers pituitary and all remarks
of a silence, you could treat them spassiparous even if
cloaking along in the dunk, it's apparent beyond making much of
the slow bricktruck of ice in assembled lozenges, my only
green and wood string temper, rides the terrier to a mildness
we have to get into this, all this, stuck up businesses
here and big birds nests on top of the telephone posts
use your icicles

Use your fingernail with these other people in pieces
of a like cranberry tapped into something that's turning here
a perimeter of windmill sharkskin greatload, smile
that the earth mounds snowed the air is good around
coat hanger light poles and do they talk? I'm going to
have to get more serious, Elvin, put on your
as our bus leads a double cross, slots here for everyone?
bricks going over sky steels, itself red as how can the nose?

Triangles all over this snow, that one knows who he is that
lives down by the sticks where his house of wood crosses by the rail
at the line, but it's yellow today closed, those woods are
timely I could then be brought back hungry from the mirror
delays these woods, steals their crosses for party passes
we canceled still, heavily the night and forward the parts
our looseness come home to in chunks, wheatbelt overpass
I only imagined were waving their oranges, fat as the sun went

Winter wonder sudden at the beach coast hotel of lace streets
white coatings
all to be crest left off alive under the marquee, brains of a moon
how long will it last how deep by morning what plan
come bump beyond one more line to become ignoramuses?
the party took our rooms, tuned them fine into carelessnesses
so to the beach at the end of a twig in snow
coats of, where is the water? coast at night, bring

Yells, look at the mirror box, hang forward if its notions
draft for an idea, at the rim box, outside on the snow part
we'll see it, the part of whom? the snort of Danish kings?
did a revolution disappear around the corner before this Peter
could see but could hear?
awful sure, as if it's night, awful cold, thought

of it as full of beer the sea, the thud
of waltzes, the mood askance of love, the tied
light, under lacing of steel, the aimed heart
splashed bronze cake with neon paints in kind of
the splendid, the hidden, the northern playing out of a Bemsha Swing
cold dish of the flake coast, they will bow
did they know?

IX.

This place now we woke to, what's up in?
could crowd down come to the meetings of
here at the Liar Farm it falls nine to the foot
parting homonyms of autumn on my mind, its leaves
whatever was left but I don't know they played it
last night's chance, the bulge in ebony walled in
and terrible tendencies of impossible movies
you walk in on a ladder in progress
the lakes in the lobbies, the women of parting
insulated dream in sections or dratted vaults
went by it all too fast so couldn't
seemed like the Centrifugal Ball of the Fire Berries
all arise to the pill supports of fire, names of in the air
another phonebooth has fallen

This place we woke to some sort of soap subsiding
to its dish of
form, or warm with its own breezes' beams?
so we don't have vastness, we have coffee
and part networks of arched instructions, to cellar that
home on over the house, word structure as part of the vista
I doubt I suppose and know something else has fallen
the verb from the sun in its trying?
the painting from the ledge in its powders
dots the plain, and our plans are up though vague
and by the bush, a demiurge in every phonebooth

Or the owner knows not which way to turn, there's a denseness
a dark horn with instructions, passes
what are the words to this cursed turn, by the platterful

the riper songforms tossed down the parcel hole of
freight flight imagination, you'd have to of course come
back from Doubt in Full, the lobby contains
Mural of Lightning
Mural of the Black Hole

Perhaps wasn't that bad a movie, of the light group comprising
Swan Steel, Music of Silver Spikes, Songs of Exhausting People
Eyegraph Boy, Snake Wanta Hold It?, Rock 'n' Roll Is Out
The Art of Big Quiet, It Snowed On My Moving, Another Fallen Down Man
Damaged Ones Talking, People Fishing With Stones, Farm Bat Legend
I Have Brought My Bandages, people walking in store-bound blocks
we walk these creased rows in the latest knees, low to the
better to be brought to you hungry with
what they said were nothing but the commonest of adders children witness

I have an address, a restaurant, an evening afternoon of
gleaming sides, powder illumined with round glass
windows the better to look at the sea, avid and cold sometimes
a lot of the man goes in to the chest, he is polar
there are apt smiles, then they go off with hoop gestures
red over their handbags, but we lie here above the sea
in a pewter gallery vinegar-locked the wines as standing lamps
desultory talks not the point, the glass price is that wave edge
beyond which charming man drowns, he doesn't but we doubt
this emptiness as bright as I want to be sincere
blind the door, far the way

It's all there in gemmy steplights
she does up the candies of her blouse front waiting
I come to a nod to see, repeat
I down my slack ale
high in oceanlight above the present

or we'll walk over candelabras
fixing up the white ones with matching socks
Live in the Dome of the Aquarium, the sea turn to a standing loan
so strolling by could walk on it

But I'm still alive but I don't know why I'm still
the answer: use one long word you get charged for two
and the elevator that snaps, I never thought to stay
was just passing, and stayed since
Lenin's Ideas Bring Good Things To Light
to mistranslate the signs, roll about the tops
where you have to wait for the statues
anything of height, on the outside of this hotel
a Bontecou of stone

Since when you start writing you drift
they march forth until a solid brandy forms
alarm and alert enough, if not avid, rigged so
war shimmers in a red glass for the sentiment
in van windows the color green of the bottom
few inches of the never-changed tank he's
alright inside

The Silicone and Graphite Hotel we hear
a rapping of scow leads as if a tangle of basements
in which a work on the bare device there needs
be, from roofs loads, down on people so slow, wait
till time, a particular orb of gel fixed lit
the men around it day and blue with short hammers
make stabs, and a certain blonde curls with fire engine lip tone

We rigged it up so she'd say that
duck fleets are coming, take four story smokes

in the dream it's all streetcars and snow but here
the wooden neighborhoods, certain greeting like a lash
to a post, the sidewalk to remember, roles to fish for
assignment: marry her and the long turn beams cold to the corner
more, poor, a tale of iced diamonds and beetle monotony
you start writing and fan your lips, start a fence, elaborate
the fight through backyards, squeak the bike tears, stained groups
the pigments all off a hue, factories without sun

Probably
they hear sex hums in the doors where
the weight of clothes in the area have
the cellar have the no-color walls almost
where nearly it won't matter what
has

But does, from the last pipe of the snow-color train
electrical near its reaches, pounds in the shuttle
won't you move over, but what are the cellars
how cement the cupola undertowers, capable the tractor sweeps
the gum off the snow, the lights off a millinery artillery
a girl in red runs on park paths

She runs on, the fall dropping, all white things giving
arrangement of Zero and the Exceptions, try to mark the place of
her stance with a dime, she skipped, all stop, all on sand
a traffic booth is raised on a stairway full to the stars
remark stars that, what's else here, the advantages of the Soviets
withholding lousy car gas, can't run, can't fly, cow out of hand
do we give them what we used to stand for?
the tower is raised
a touted barrier, erected snail, brash, all

But trapezius juice stands, by which they go
clinging to the diva of wooden outline, Margaret Whiting
maybe a change of spread, of delicious stars who in bending
become artists remaining sneak thieves of a partial paradiso
turning losses high into rain gears, has sports gone
big in its reaches, he leans to apply this snare
lower in their catches, then this white-out stops the talk

Care to repeat that radio? nothing better to see
than in oldtown a fallen down man some passers help up
twice, like a thrown load, by the barter lamps of gold corner
juice brigands tarry there after helping hats, another portion did it
he laid, not for long though she yelled, must've been known
I seed, she backed his every, we moved on, nothing was still

Blue screeds, zone of arias?
another light of after river to a smoking infinity, sign of a wrench
accordion to her, and we turn on our street in the snow branch
kilter of hard awning hotel, Petrarch's home studio
flat broke a minute but handy, a certain tendency to horses waiting
for frozen streetlamps that work though, a girl
whose head is wired carrying cubes
near the squash yellow wall interminable honey
of a tropical stripe the electrical shack so now everyone's backing out
I wouldn't be sorry be sure

As in audiences, advantages
of the endlessly funny this one talks and turns tail
as if it's going to charm people, stuff it in your drawer
then if you could read and soar, good enough, can it
grow of an illness the strongest of questions, armchair to follow
and yellow dolls in the head, the barrel of the master box
seat in which my knees get bent, his ping-pong and his snow
and I wouldn't limit a thing without tears

Would you jam with the evil dead in a dark and frying hand
gloat of club, take your coat, walk a batch, it all ticks
where they corral us lay out the foods space a few live on lead
went classically portly in the October and bore war brands freeze
and tape about the head, some of us vanish, some front the grill
of a martial drum machine, its erasers on matchsticks
the hollow barrels of the weight kids or Lester Lanin on Percodan
a shade shover
we were not held over, came home pet faced from his fate class
so the high spark of the low hum guitarist echos on the cuff
a terrorist love cat, and stacks his whistles and hums his paper plates

Then pick our low midnight, and even a bit past it
ship back on the pole bus, snow budge, sky clear to the stars
curblight backs blink the way, the miles of bridges
and I think this hotel too blinks

X.

Now that orange stripe now not
nor longer an orange stripe that once
did have the orange stripe but don't
what was an orange stripe now isn't
given the orange stripe no other
orange the stripe of this wall top missed
the orange stripe of a wall so gone

But pocks of snow, every way
everything was, over all
it will no longer be?
no longer my desire to get things right
to stop and be pleased to snap
no matter the whole of the film of play is
to pretend to be out of film and really be
crossing rivers Riga
frozen fencing Riga
duck brigades Riga
Riga of the lit blue globe held by the three men

Once I finally got it right I stopped
in which this is enclosed
where the name of a peace is the same as the world
they have signed to each other and not sent cables
the word has bubbles contain others
to the teeth

But we are the Beach People
some others are the people who live in cement
the same word for wire or wolf, do they call?

what is your name in Wolf? down at the chain snap lounge
Riga of the burning black steeple of the golden rooster
rings beneath in vault with sagging ash arches and the spark below
the burst
where said jazz club spreads for us, knocking things like bells in a frame
do they lodge? where we shop in colored light where it's impossible
to leave this world, it's impossible weight trailing weight
to move over and score all this for kerosene tongs and a wineglass
obscured by a signal, and it is a Baltic signal

Unusual lot of striped room and a slight object
these people become violent on streetcars, how covered their will?
they don't want things they want to hold on
arms straight out as rods to represent the pigeons huge
and frosted though unlit, as the big guys rise and pretty women
fossilized, the alcohol, the curbstones, salesmen, like that?
I could stride to the salt threads of innards
and bunk till the main is made?
business all combined on a street with lashed vests and worsted
the buckling trolleys mount to their last face lightly spread
a lot cast to the front of all owed needs?
or spinal, you see it there throwing
the man's back to the sound of its shears as he passes shut
the budged vitamins of an unwitting spill
the skull core and brash container
hands on a pet and hounded luck

Death
in the woods
where it is quiet for the shots
the death
where it is
the heart in its box tocks

to the camp, to cement, to the earth
the quiet of ones
their rung slab under, that waiting
go

The box in which the members are told be heros
in the field kept clear, of ladders and stars
the box in which no speech was saved
in the field of a uniform
box of a clamp
cold spread field of a rising dark
where the box of mad market so fits
the field of no light, backed with smoke in no hands
the box of mechanical blooding,
the field that has always existed, will ever show flat
the box in waiting, that I will always hate it
the field wide box shut stands and the cold
in the ground is enough

And driven there in buses and let out
and driven back through the black market of cars
and driven back through the eventual afternoon light of factories'
windows
everywhere everyday everytime
the dice cut open

The death of all that difference is the loss
the permanence of that death is the mystery
a feeling for the woods in deep change
the blood flies as the crystal drops
and thought we heard wolves

He wants a young and beautiful life

Meanwhile, the step right up to the blue sky
no stretch from trains I'd forgotten about
the overwhelming factory smoke, rhymes with snow
to block letters on everything, the subsequent wall grindings
forest green and brick red the ones
switching engines and grey of the box, to see
cement bears exposed wiring well
but frustrated ochre walls, to not
break in our bent, rhymes with snow

Blue and white and cement so occasional polygonal
color patches the human wait on stone
subside to freeze in everywhere, a doll-humid thunder in the way
we trench beneath to wait out that television blade
makes a tomb for the sky, down here we escape at night
where go forwards backwards, as does snow the sky
still sticks to sticks and these kids

Live in a kerosene nightmare, in streetlamps'
cod-liver oil, that map under the rug and pile a chair over
too still to dream, steal out from edges, a man's barrel rolls
the round black hatch slows to reveal, rayon drums
all vertical and in colors you smell when you edit
erasure flaps well spun, grit oars once come to shore
once tabled under the time statues

But the very name studio means we want to be taken
by the fine thin so beautiful wants
his life tuned to a certain standing, we are watching
as we're hauled over motion over roofs our play
the payback of painters, coal fire and drain
tea till it pinches, a coat tail of spent duck
the lockout of matches, neon down the separate stairs

in drapes and legs of addresses of edits all over
the pace of a brought repast in a backroom tower
with lit chat as the sun stalls in its own smoke
over a pigeon river, it gets bluer later

But are we wise, or do get feels from cold
courts and square dusk walks, crowd trolleys to outskirts
where silent exit waits, sever-blue points at the wrist
over orange damage blocks, it's to witness on a run
from studio grounds to back fence heard near a rug beater
or on iced tracks and never in years the yellow ash of samizdat heaven

Where everything permitted nothing sanitized, the latest issue handed
over its crushed seeds between sheets, inflatable politics bags
and more that the sex is printed black masked back and with arrows
you arrange your rejoinder from the rear and very well it snaps
on the smaller drum, the one collided from camera shells
the blade in its fluids all bone to roll out dead
we find the building of wolves the bats have had the girl to pieces
does she bother? her feet into high heels turned
then drawn and burned she offers him a light as her head deletes
coffee streaming, hair to rise, bone up the front and bare behind
it's all bleeding on the buildings, over battlements from stars of ink
rot, next will be corroded the copper cage with ruby lights

I stuck it back where they had me, definitely what's brought me
the gaze of Art Blakey under Saint Basil's jolt of question
how quick is the fuck allowed shattered, the way the shot breaks
can't read but can see, the one sprawls open there
smiling shut her eyes
can you see me?

Just the slightest of clothings and the steeple tips and ducks flash
upward to the reversed street of crossed cigars and the rumor is
the best is of someone pushed, the spirits flying right from
the burn button
and no music lost to the felt of cold toques, or sailcloth of
a pickup angel out on loan
no one to break the arc

A hasty one
the torque-driven ballast eggs in sun
of the wind-driven pylons don't touch
the radiums in the bath, it's reach
power of a double state whose room
totals it in the rest of it
a silence scorched it down

These are little pocket innuendos for the power troopers
give a hidden dawn its papers you've ended
properly the iced inks? I am alone on sulfates
so no book stalls where I honk, swap goggles for a scarf
link passing handles as sky drifts in a cabbage rose
and now I pretend home and now these shoes have walked on the moon

This is all by fast by splinter puff and beckon
backward in the hatch of things, a harp mystery of boiled postcards
echoed mantis placed the tools, apt for penetration sudden
loveliness in orange nearer and ground to the glasses
under iron teas, this strap is chained to my last habits

Founded this town was invention of the lag bolt
by the zen monks in furs bopping each other so fast
it is impossible to wince
caught in a clock so ding, the whole town to

up and rinse down to the earliest shovel follower
a park of short hands it is

I know the lines
I just can't sign to this ceiling
a tin vintner and rubber syrups, miraculous
how much blowing can stop, I signed myself out
the way of the rusted soups, the marriage of whole fields
to a can of beans, for example needed trial
then syphoned camphor into a glare, but do I know
enough to stop being here? is it the elevator
which burned and a fog horn that reaches?

A quarter of elephant lemon in a brine gong glass, laughter
even on another tongue, let the level of my sea be kept
in wallet stone on bribed edges, these are branded things
dropped

Near quote's end
is the earth's inner nest a char or a tongue
of clear inertia? these ones
all fitted together like shelves
the anyone else's followers hated
though whoever makes it happen makes it
blue or reddens it later however the hang of it goes
the gold hatters then turn mad? the butters
who rent the garbage crevasse speak breakfast at what?
just a bit of amethyst insanity in the hallway?
and with right bitter turrets closing spawn the mate
of cubical crystals from mud of many's the mold on one wall
you'd never have to waltz at all, like
coming home chipless in full monsoon?
your cost is my win

Decimal in fact he said from the roof where he's sweeping the snow off
does it follow then that those pigeon beads will follow?
people there woke back and laid it on for us, shooting labels
and gaberdine eggshells, the light put out in the collider
did Ernie Kovacs? overly familiar stays at Mount Sumpter
where did that parlor aim its back juice, or a price
for which those strings will stray from normalcy
lace like cake in a wound, a cable takes grain off stars
it's an edge you can storm from didn't she hold?
the one who hitched then laughed at the coffee perimeter
where bathroom glass and old lungs, pestles and lean
carburetor strands
I set down the talc limiter and watched old iron sway

XI.

Or threat was a dream? or is it result of
unfashionable thimble we got home we found
a turned room and whole house further long
shaken the cement to pink fists and bland
a block factory for pulling plastic fragment goods in threads
I approach him in the distance over the pebbled glass transition
as dream runs out of space, a broken gaze, and wake

Earlier
remains earlier
been trying something heavier before flowing from the dream
don't trouble the ones, leave them shifting wants and doubling for
she'll have me to let her try out her, and other samples oriented
one on me, a further crossing brought out on thought
for a try past the dream, its zones of speed and slide
to a halting blurt and short of her glasses, crossing on a throat
of song, Cross Over the Bridge, and not to think of it since now
the first time here, which remains bright and rare to be
a name all out of chords, but bridges are not that rare
it's just that all the bridges are here

On the road to the talk of a creek called Age
a man takes the snow apart inside a fish called age
or mandolin, I've never done things, and then
I've never done better things, don't play, just wipe
the wrists to come out in airs, did we go?
but it's a sand that we need but white like the weather
and slow enough to write, or write to a telephone somewhere
out here a people aware of the hardness of the frame

Sounds like they said, No place of boards where it's full up
sorry? just squint your eyes, don't worry out the side
it's all storing on, finding without slowing
the needlescent golf grounds
on a snow tour of the phone poles a deuterium residue
in feathers peeling off that puff the bird away, besides
it's called pragmatism, the screw cap on a valve box
boosterism, a recidivism played so vile it smells of cello
or a heart so knitted it makes three beats of one
but between those trees no one needs, is that harmful
or just colorful, and now it's got too silly, poor reception
of the repetitious glance, the one is afraid of the snow
the other fears to see it on the sea
and we who remain have yet to see a thing

And I who responded, a quiver of lights
bucket of window radar waving lands
a tool so fleet I can't see the day, so I'll move
but the dream so based it stays, lowers well
can't cap its face so come down in particles
a stubble clown, the aisles of his talk to the whiteside, done-to
there is no waved-on winter without its replacement field
cold flights snap, birds hedge, I'm more
the imposter the more I can

Triangles the gaps in slender farms, there are plurals
of course off the map, roaring away in afterthought
for those who have no alphabet, will the grey
that's really blue come through this brown that's really white?
a track where you lost the time, continue, remove
your face from your mouth, when growing up lock
a hand, three hearts, a ladder up a tree
from which to valentine that gap in the tinsel forest

short of everything man shaves a few clicks, man walks to
dump truck, so we played
on the way wove your hair in the show of small fallings
put and take and pull all your friends together
where lands a feather, the sea is a graywacke

Don't you, won't you know anything, while stopping
I can't, writing
my nerves won't move in this angle of a fix
the need to is risen and telling, I wasn't held up
so I stood out, caught where this leads me, head of a vast
I couldn't go out cause he wouldn't be there, he has
a place he stays but I couldn't go anywhere he was
it's too comfortable staying liftable, shook out plain in the raise
this hourly fight it stirs us to put, the craft pulling over
the sheet on a shelf and drop your shirt, it lives but
I'll have to write bigger or larger faster so quick it needs
be a clown for to caliper that dot, preposterous period
they're not wanted, as long as you won't be responsible for the winter
then build, say, a terrible set, say, but bigger

The trees are a child terror, then Uncle Ink comes
and saves the dice, by the lake of barrel stares in
noun temple band we touch lakes, our mirror going totally by
things on top of other things but with no attachment
the mirror oiling no dial in its ice
these trees cap a cold doll hour
tenderly, the committed atrocity
then the band sits down

To the one I'd have to pin a steam hat to
the back of a tablecloth clock, see, even
parsing it on wheels by the wheel, low

edging rows the roars, then get out by
the sea in the snow
mind

Where you can see the matter
go white inhaling its oxygen
the wind held to nothing but
its vanishing compound, he is leaning
against this giant cinder
that is flat out paying for all we have done
so we gain in shouts and grow hand springs
once he has gone some way to that place he stays
we replace him with distance, then like a name returns
in covering study on the head of Driftology
or scintillant member of the eyes on hand
drill a wrench through thin beach, pipe China
sprain a ruckus, freeze this boulder to the helmet's head

The coffee's hard and so is the cream, in layers
so is this morning, all I had to head away from
frozen, not that everything will interrupt this, float
found a head in the sand, strips of lung, a suspended
auto by the snow field highway, how do we rate hanging
these frosts of connection, a place-taker, mild farmer
might mention, no, these are the snow wires
at the Last Visage, taut front

It makes its mark on the backyard shore
where a pluck feels like a flout
and octopi now span the macaroni
in a giggling slip slated to gather same but got whipped
allowed as far as the lobby for this, all these tarts in white
sprung in the bar of the no-lunge museum, short cream in waves
adroit, then went out and got the fury in trouble

It was a green Model T, be sensible

Of you I sleep, and watch it

Cheese arrives on this road at all the curves
hails from the pea-green planet, on average
they'd let him pace for four days then put him away
that that note got ripped on the blind side
a dog would halt

The rest is out and out literature of the few
and all carrying crosses and pulling things off, entered
the cavern of useless lights, flew free from the word palace
could I then be the Head of All Reality?
still a thing to bet on, watch for
of you I sleep
I'll call you up as soon as the road's back

Keeps whiting my land
back, how Russia is it?
nobody's favored with
the life to play stable
awful how into it the friends are but otherwise
notes by Alma Coma
how caked brown and intimate the arsenal

Just do
one pair of the many thing
or end up let to
the further place where pulse and choice do go
the openers put their own limits
then if you can get beyond
fine, the materials go

I'd love to get beyond fine
to frame all this in its zone of force free
no
these the Impedimenta of Protected Scratch
the sorrows of the player exhausted beyond his backyard
just what is this, is his?
not that I doubt the planners of this balloon twilight
enough to budge a ride
enough to shoebox any size sound
in a shortening
with strings

Need more logic in the background so we could play it longer
these meters could use some banana daylight
less facade cement and grease plan spuds
a novel of it all of nouns, believe

Get dry so ride lifts to a meanness
get hard eyes to travel with, the normal slant of time is gone
as the creaking sign of heaven fans breath to tan the stone
they get wall drunk and cut the wind with their glasses

And then the wind cracks, where is the hallway
where will it matter that way
we hear them racing the wheels out there in
arctic plies around corner room wind stops
their trades, bristling with lit cigs, brown shag nation
about a pearl on the market or session in lead casino
took from lab jacket pocket, a slow smile

In here the exact timings are down on it, sauce in hand
have you felt the snare? spun in the veins of neighboring beacons
the power of this planet is harbored in devices like glasses and red
but Braxton's dotted feeling is from the way he tongues it
once got home shut a hole, truck revs like cutting cabbage
since everything you're held in is total slab
if I never could stand it I would surely have it here

Then a sheer howl comes by, followed by a scrape
hummed to the brine of animal pretension, a whisk at the map
indication of scour by no light on any panel, he hustled to
witness loud exclusion, a separate occasion only
they went to parallel bars

Why don't they rebuild the death barracks out of lead?
monumental after all that landed in the lead airplane glaring east
it's all in hurry out there where those shiny folks scrape the road
in axes and elevens, smoking Mars, barring safety
the single thing will carry you, alarming harp or organ down
the useless white stairway, broad of a cost pressed into
pectoral station where excess gas is caught we're entrenched
as viewers Cyrillic Mickeys in the early, creaky green neon
might get home after
which lights or some winter here

The bread made of brass
or get a whirling education at the edge of this building
a guessed entrance to the winter night
just the eastern one, played out then in
scow moons and cow bales
once the thump against purest paint takes
this one wall
bitterest spare of our salvages

XII.

Gull drawn in
red wheels
dawn beyond
hung stockings

Seize you in hours, thigh zone gauze complete
street about the car start, a dense trance Baluga
or a Moriarty extent committing
something something expendable
this nodule boot bucket chance of barest Russia

What you had been thinking about a whistle blew shrilly
where the western hem line is a lettuce signal
got a trade without a sample
mule jumped on veins in your screening permit
signed, Thorstein Veblen
signed, Henry Threadgill

There is no space, there is nothing
but
old stone towers, spacings of windows in walls
just
dug samples of harm on the average, horn in
thoughts to buy
at Braxton's Thump, where I thought the red line jumped back
where I thought of the union of throttle union and throttle unison
sat in his room and thought about his trees
up above his thoughts bebop, salt
and what could have been the thought lesson for this grace?
before the attitudes came down, before the paper town lasting

thoughts that know not but the joy of case
bummers in strings that his ace travels well
in case in keeping
these thoughts I hoped
I hadn't misunderapprehended
Time Was

Some tables
prepared to look away
from all angles, some tables
prepared to listen to
themselves then yell, no doubt
some mostly don't, these tables tasks
for a supper prepared as if on Mars

XIII.

Nowhere last night was more dramatic
snow for a while on the bus to nowhere
blue gap morning clear less cold
an old enough town to miraculously eat
without language, to slosh it around in the bottom
of what were my dreams, which way to dry?
what are the simplest means? gone with
the suspension of storms, this time
we will reach, we will match
a non-magnetic scotty by the side
the parallel journey that was fear

Is he doing what right?
the oblivion then was fir
the highway itself was a firm
fog-sped lowlane Siberia high night
kept turning by hay racks, moose and horn
were we hidden there saying it's true
we catch other moods with no warning in the seat?
was the violet dog on the right and were we shown?

I hear the clicks as the blocks snap back
together they are tiny, the night crawls
thereby sings to a stop, in every way bizarre
the rule for these encounters, those with the gallant
beards are brave, it says, it dots these rumors
lets go back in a philological stupor
but you can't go stay there, no star to speak
no gunpowder bubble that bursts once past
the cathode arch of bricks
she has read them

And encounter the chins, young and in blends
all you could hope to rest from, and stop eating fruit
in reddish slabs, a form of house that rents
that could fade it all back into laps of perpetual afternoon
unless night, stop calling it in case
by case, a motor kicking up in the snow
to a halt, a brush with, animals move
unless the sky is not raised. enough
but we're high, look at those cones
drop from the air

Stub, he
it's gone
and the air is marked with a question point
in a circle, but is
this seat trip the plural leap you wanted
please
to be polished to a copper square by key roosters
spare parts to our sunday, a cousin of the theater Russian
cleared them, Icky Part rockstar, he lives up over
everybody must have been a spy, but that's America
ask him
he does Liza in many forms

Does this plane work?
it's a long way to quote
airs from this bag of snow
own wants
can you handle the tracks
an army of sound
like the sun in slats
and I quote, we leave
then walk in a group a long way across

to a spot that's left
of slow steps, canceled forms and the ramp

It's a dump, and was mean
I mean solid, says the coming moron
in layers of silver species, they raise in saying
and don't go off in the sky, though there are
places where the spells

A washer, just a washer

Housing the several planes of Cool Ludwig
in the land of the collective clouds
have I come back around aware or sore awake?
the national octopi of specific TV
first real then cartoon?

The foot then the carbon
was a place we could start numbering back from
cool old machine in a dive that morning
waves
that lines the sorts, then the color
then the cover ends, is brightening?

Have you got a balance wheel on this?
in a huge claustrophobic area
nozzle first base room, remembering Finland Station
and big like open zones on claustrophobic cues
a real apology in back of where the clouds came awake
the burgers wouldn't leave, alone
I imagine chaired by
what was lost stops
what regained stays

Instead of the forest dark a big jelly field
fraught ends at the polution of money, honey
what is planned gets wholesome, the rest tends to dark
do you think? are you filled with mood?
arriving clear on a bunch of rhythm, and then lost
the waiters who wouldn't applaud wouldn't leave
as we were flown all across that floor
it lasted

The secret of donut dough, what occurs to
tin cars with plastic keys, of tone forms
with Abulafia hats, their hurried remedies
of Bobolink Airlines, will we be let go
or stored with the brews that left us here
is he doing what in the night?
this briar calm of wound things

The secrets are
be tides, masts in twist and noisy tents
decided things, all furled across the rest we have to go
an oath, and then more sun, then sure
if you are reading thinking this a code, it is
but only to be read up into further codes
is said, there is an ultimate outer
precariousmost position, then put her there
then light on you

Fractal field by fractal estuary, a totally
unfolded geometry, crystals on glass of glass
grown vastly arctic, sheets no rod applies
bestows of iron no stored overnights
then feeling weird and wanting to be liked
this snoring horse follower plugs his puts his dad
right in the mouth and well, goodnight

Air of home doesn't have that sort of major deposit
plastic curse, gulch vat, hair of henna and a diamond wing
where we sit in thrones and harvest the tempo of (a) what
that rhymes with the outer geometry and (b) whims and spoke ratios
no grabirons, no marsh gas ghostly folds, no rules
only a stem or two offered by those of ginger legs and stick
only remember later, when the sun goes I must have my knees
their lakes and offer resemblances, those globe-headed bicyclists
that light on the ride and blink at the light

Have grown vast, the time to be dressed and thinking of
an iced lake for breakfast placed and dated if hung before
I don't believe you but all the persons wearing suits of grey
and slugging, from the shade by the lots of waters pale chains
and fighting not to touch their scratches, so told the increase
in hand, dawn a coin

Finally to be away, straight from the somebody who talks that much
we must assume the sun, even rain and ceiling of bald stars
the market of all this never idle, almost married, sad throughout
I think that was A. Artaud driving that taxi, his face lit from beneath
around the dead grass rims of the co-op turnout where nobody plays
clarinet
or fishes with stolen pins, then he does and says, in other words appears
to come in from the stance he throws, leaning in grey strides
from the opposite heaven
my parents came from the red lakes, a plate with no light, a snap
and then some polemics will make you blind, avoid vibration
and vending the live ambiguity traits to an audience of stones
they raise to grits, dust rules and it's all brought flat

Would it be possible to find something to eat in this dream?
in the Ultimate Afternoon of Stores, apparition severs out to

the insular predicament of quartet, what did you see in to say?
is this a preparation for Water Trend Magazine with its stills?
many years he could hold the drill all dull, a picture issue in which
Jack Benny plays his suit, looks to one Berman's handheld shots, sulks
somehow managed to space the stairs, still they call
to talk poetry or the chaos of physics, but barely a numb magazine

Is my poetry home? no, but will also
include parts of one river, one stable, one
harmolodic trust

Neat
marbleized standards
they observe here
Klaatu, barada, nikto
raised in perfect order
the precessions of Gort

After all this transparent complaint he was a kind
of Johnny OneTone at the airplane curtain
contains that grey is a uniform thread
of many silver rings the cardboard in this sky

We are
and know what we knew we are
space, space, and some space
left
alarmed at the start of the lighter
kites, rafts, that trembling
comes only in flash dreams

Salts assumptions of our looniness to the grain
Moscow will have windows and a border of dust

included in the code of thoughts, will it predate dreams?
what lurks included in the code of balsa, low intensity loaves?
thought in dull whine then under dark bulb in bus aisle
recalling each syllable in Lush Life as the juice peters out
through the road its socket
why were we in love with those lamps? as if in such a turning
all our words went landed and duly matched, a hard habit to be simple
to be single, to bring home the notches from trees

Moscow with its heavens closed
on launch days, a shade of wood come to cover
for those sprung patches, the grain to their blues
just a thought someone has got up and used
but stay, not yet

We must needs discuss the poetry life deep through bone intensity night
no UFOs, no sense of a thing uniform that trembles in plan
to come before us whole but lazy, no curtains
the spouting before the made crash
we peer from aisles to see, lifelong if inverted, high across the colder
east
of us, okay to have invented those forms, but what when
we have come to the perimeter cones?

Crisscross mixed with jet trails down a mountainside
there are none here along the tone roads, foulard in a clamp
I had my repast, you your foreign airspace
are you finished or is there another object?

Lands, paradise, bare and breezy radar of peppermint
they had them in their labs there loose when alone he leaves the building
a building of low ceiling in which the perpetual snow blows
blue stares, icicles in the crystal, and how many did he know

in perfect or relative keys, where perfection is pronounced
among the darker pyrites, nodules buried deeper in their desks so you
please paradise, hand me, let me follow
that yellow Pinto blinking to relieve
any old ice of its setting
Moscow is

Moscow is drinking irons and the tell of a purple river
its drains to unlatch Alaska and low enough oblongs
a bolder broadway in declarative sentence raked over the orebody pines
a snap of wooden crystals cures your loaf, standing man
to move
to link
a slower breathing high
old tempo order of the dance, palms tapping heels
an ageless tendentious simulacrum of tires in the workers' tired knees
told as the cigarette of a darker bread in breathing closes
stone admits, the heavy aisles so lit behind that we turned
but the band pronounced it prunes, an aversion of locks
would you want it, let's live blindly, the art of Parenthesis
Vodka

The noise of the vodka, or river, tapped out on the radar
of a time

Keeping time on radar
in a brick square
in the snow backs
from the zero light
degrees of scarlet
stars of points
to Zambonis flush and the candy towers
racks of auto

the hot cut sentry
wakes, stand around and
he hears Polaris tapping

How to cross where avenue means
width extreme? wait for the trees, he claims
his brain timing roars of the light hot passageway
Alabama limo on the avenue, cross wires, pronounce
and leave

The way to the next

Chain of enablement blocks with frequency
aim a hair off though, rubies to glow on spires
tread the witness stairs tractor by leftover subway tractor
a bothersomeness collective in lines across
where turrets end and snow smells as lead divides
an absolute roughness and further, and coded normal
even spoke, searchlights their roots in snow, the haste
beams up in rose and blue before the gathering tomb turns
I have salvaged it in, his thought to say
tanks along avenues in the balance that wakes
red what?

Something going off where they're showing him things
in example as an F-hole in a pancake, long division
and more or less the start of time or stop
the stars, where?

Moscow is huge with blinders, coal roof blowers
those graveless blinkers, the men who made up
all those rules laid out today, the grind of that
whoevers of this mauve and thick hotel slam a door how many times

may now look in print the things, before
they kept bringing him back until the physics wore out
now pulls the denims of how many numbers to the sheaf
their cards after all ballistic, tones of false sides to the head
erased nail file, say, row of sables by a cabin, say
count until their radio sounds
people ride in a hole in the ground, sing

I make a move as if to quarry the granite but really
emphatic wooden books in cases of the cloth so easily suspend
and I mean
the loops under those billiards made of cattle washers
when the marble's too busy being then back home we'll
have to lift this all again to a metro maximum
a run on those carrot carriers, linkers to go
and the only xerox nobody's allowed to use
raise
bricks with the nails driven between them
bloom

XIV.

Moscow gives
green steel mirrors in the morning closet
a language out of air, largeness of flint
layers of rusty decking parts, might be
a collision we had, these words

Kept on the bone, made their problems grow tame
but which one was his and which left?
Moscow grew
brassy and flown, must stay to keep
old hat in secret closets

Dreams of girl France in wedgewood academies
of the mood, a thundercloth over, with
bookrack Larries and beholden buses long
the flowered stone, why won't you? and on
we spin between
book wheels to get in

This was a sun but now
klaxon metronome, crooked top hat
in meal jar, electrolytes to China hard
nibbling away at the pewter cherry, antimatter piranha
flames fall into snow, syrup again entire
and there were three of them correcting the hangers of coats
cooperating teaspoons in Kafka's remaining cracks
it serves, so open my meaning, no corporate
chunk elaboration, terse an error I could not

Slung a man who would bag himself for

Horseback hinges into the glovers' lives

Open moon in the air to tighten

A disparity of close sports, had on racks, stamps
a tangle of old rocks, the quicklime sonatina we all
and what else but that one the lie will kill
soap crystallizing while
ores suspended a discussing tour
length on a guy's length
bores

You wanted all the octagonal colors for yourself until you grasped
a man and an effeminate woman arguing over a hole
in the ground in the snow
this story to take, this smoke over the Moscow blows
the sun to shreds, two shreds
you counted all the sideboard ledges, their gingham damps
the lengths one would go to pull down

Furs on arms in the dark
or arms in a darker hole
firm as an arrow in a metal rocker
they're just like laborers everywhere
any old way you
bend into line
my weighted favor, your manner of park
any bold thinning of the line

The made-up thing in any brick yard
flak punk echoing
the chip that went missing
the reason

But in dramas of a high solidarity the families
take the kids off in trucks through rock tunnels
it all ends in a hate, a thread hat by some scored slabs
it's night again and here are the bad guy and horse animations
large-as-a-magazine white ones, central with stain
the committee totals a nation's chances
bear copper flags across the borne walls

And walks in a rage of coats, surviving, looting trades
talking to nobody without a hat, and they all but don't, I live
in a setting with fire in place, seated, ear flap array
in fact a tear tour with perpetual snowplow and shovel
as many who are here do, evaporate, prepared, be right
and says settle in the escape-proof afternoon, gunning for snail
it's a day, a day late and she makes a goblin sound

Threatening to tour then rushing in with cold Lenin I await
tumbling by the mounds where they keep, balancing, told to wear
and I stop, we care, and the museums roll by, it's all kept
believing, stained and leaning, the wave of huge blocks
and I'm stumped, deride, assay, Pushkin with Impressionists
say, now are the Sparrow Hills, they stare, we are in place
another view heaved by, startle, curlicue, window

All rises, ands with hats potted, and I learn as I
ski jump plate with outdoor pool stone bubble pad steams
we live by the steams, your rooted heating plant dives in to tell
and browns, and capable to the luxurious, renting and the buckles clog
click, he's thinking how Moscow smokes, converts its contents
a deep blue ink to a sort of crimson gum, course it is so cold
emission time but we are too, I like, she turns and the snore
coupling the mad, tied to scant, the man's head in a frosted box

Balancing on the snow black shine of the carrot cannon's tip
he laces, stirring, not able to be known, carouse, sighting
and land, its even turns, the cold turns now, my eye
my loans, coming, commenced, alert to what tips to trick
we relate return, stopping the smokes with an ice snap
he's concluded the shop with nothing
so last on the tour within is seen
tree pinkness of the black exchange

He sings shrugging, leather engaged, will last to the touch
with its granite pins, Moscow regular, pleased at a sitting
May friend's gift, a piece of pliers, labradorite tomb lock
half-life to anyone's reign, tonal radiates, they scour them then
as if freed of, as if off and ranting, a dollar a whatever
doesn't look like, here it's wire returns weaving and not
of a stripe won't stick with the convent of the fox

Moscow's strain, a parrot cell in a goblin drome
not to seeing say it won't come in touch with, lasting, combs and
the frost register commitment casino pilaster kneedip allstars
slated, and all this grey zoning, cars to carry it beyond the carts
the wholes to be awful? avenue, casement select avenue treated
avenue of cement bandbox monumental keepsake fakebook on landing
spread, a mile from the planet, will this concert, take this second
bout to make it happen, glassless and tongue out, a mirage balloon
or whole tree of golden ages of, the biter so kisser of these facades
in realm of true takes miles pills and the language is copper
or the tin from these flag banks, or what's tied to the flags

They have seen these words, or similar, so what that
pigeons drop loose to fly from anyone's arcade ceiling, the telling
in whose wrists couldn't match you, and bringing in badges away
a whole glass shirt of your front in side bars and slot averages

the tongue for the bulk though tiny you'd have, though lit precise
the lineage velvet electric geriatrics: of that? trees will release
jack back, the X beams as far as they approached, hatching put up
go home and time that spar to its rest

More, though through no fills further, a list of the bands ignored
jumped barepate and coatless over four-foot stones of the marble freak
him missing nothing, scoping eternity in a downtown massive whole
spot where put your hands together then take them apart, coughing in
a cloud chamber preparatory and we marry but nobody bothered, classing it
middle management of no integrity, everywhere, in house or quite yet
thoughts in the bank? I haven't decided yet

Tumbling tube of the troubling majorities in the van and on charts
the weird scenes inside truth serums where anyone if short advances
in the proper sort wire glasses, stemmed, trained, avert alert
shore it up, don't think, take your shot, piss them off, remind
on rewind, the breath on hold is, and answers and double totals
the sun storms, nothing could be here, cut to last the lie, a mist

In my Moscow mirror the winter fly has died of fast fog

But on Arbeit Street, it's too cold to sing but can paint
where loose hallways are taken to thread outside, the cry beyond latch
slid along below stands for said, then had it covered indigo
doled from its fuel cell, redness is all over the pretty girl, goes
madness pretty soft, sure, many's the caught dead in tune

And loudly
you that are raising hands to thought's barn

The city occults
district sun held to district smoke
we don't build plants where the air is sound

won't hold with problems, spring bare improvements
I knew made a difference of me
but want to stand on ledges, bare fangs, make people
then raise them loose, make them do things

A pale picket fencing between the pinching buttresses
the many platforms, stylized implements
the perpetual upholstery, set out in the street and match

Don't wait, value money or gifts so shop
too much it is a crust to, the opening to mine is
a failure I open and walk

And everyone gets in, at least anyway
the one who makes a grabbing sound
scours the tumbrel of its fishskin dollars
as physics to chemistry laughs
a coffee or the soap, which is it?
this week is scarce here
what is green and splits there
but I must have the music enter
all the zones beneath this fly
and in case there are

Lost

Gains
an area beyond which could be
nothing but one sustained note

Lastness of things
but lastness continues, and I have to move the names
a bit away from things that have no names

Is all
is known
is over but it happens
to not even notice
the same time making worse

But have strange enthuses
schedules and wartimes
mandate of the biting scale barely seen
thought to move, even land and try

The one who lives off in the word stream
held seldom on visit but works out of all this vizored
one's partner particled in the blaze visitation
snapping for the score, avails one what
in murmur spelling eyes, any question
of this wait will be later
crowded to get away
left of the matter that
or of the match

And we drive away through brink sectors snapping onions
where persons spend serious time in their waits for lights
he said he didn't even notice it, he was there
high in perpetual thin effeminate forms, grinds the score
contemplates eat of the night cake
steadies to train the shapes to love
the drop of things in possibility, Moscow has
a deep green sofa and a refrigerator motor in a corner
please, the heavy drape of a wooden hoarding
information of that cosmic an indifference, send it
signed, Gap in the Sounds

XV.

The gap left behind us nothing
but overshoes and carvings with magnets and mudguards
we go befriend but we stay alack with what is
practical in a practical joke, a trembling that leans in
on intent to chew it all bending over in a steel storm on a clean street?
we are regulation and our lives are heavy
but they will not return

Leaving the masked city
what did you take it to do
cooperate with my money?
then he put it to me with bartender accuracy
that it's loud in Mineral City
which is after all the world until me
in a precision of nothing, this revision of nothing
putting it all away then taking it back in perfect part
a trick was established in hats impossible in words
meanwhile choosing to be watching
Marina Vlady in Follow Me
we were
so there

She has to comment on frozen tin window sheets
shop here?
in this battle of the pieces was the robot fruit
kept shut up against strong green ever fresh?
no, the revolution is pictures
the side of a guy's head, no story
of the woman's front, we grow parks
to line the realm's longest fences
this revolution is song

And its sizzle, bend to, the flat of the hand
trembles, then dozens and they go lark, come a leak
recompense, driven, scared as rabbit in coven weighed
we look and even if it doesn't they mark them
massive and leaning and we're taught, stored, the light
towers to an Olympic radium, going to go in there
it's right last night, finally saved, a carry on tone
at Peccary Palace up in the flow where the words teem, splay
and can I get an orange drink, or pretzel, jumping
at the mention of the vanishing amphibian, he'll never get over
the roots here, man in working cap statue, boulders three
before a last block, his knee snapped, and so moved
and so housed, a milk case to every daily thread
black vents, cannery smile, blue flow snap went on
as we went along pulling along
the lighter ones are the stallions

Fluid
pig-eyed
enchantment of choices
snowy railyards of my old days
the one red flag in all those windows

A leaving grace
leaving for the space where
the word for to speak is to blow
like act
a silliness of sign all over this town
where towel rack is the same
as the man in a wall of graphite
is the name of this town, a bent chairback
or chain of event, sanitary leading to
pussy pulled across at the top to be dispensed at the side

I'd rather clear fluorites
so
take that random kid once more through his rock formation
sock him to it, lake
take up your golf bar into an airball
have it how come we're along windows but not equal
to soon fine down if not to this cozy place?
enough, he had a struggle hole start at his face blades
it's cough required, are we fit to start? or at last
walk on by
that lake where the play hovers for one last boy and no one stares

Chi Chi, how does it go? he flew, strong as ceilings
where lots don't spring at people's approach, cold hope
for villains of such a solo, we're picked up and gone
can you finish low without breaking up? no, and so
brought jello beyond the ninja trade to Nigerian open
where treads the felt snow and aardvark means come in
world words warp transparently by
while there in your drink an ice skull
says a certain Van Cleef as Captain Arpege
comes in trouble with
another now deceased

XVI.

May be an answer but there won't be an ending
I was too slow in my blend of link to spoil and tell us
as all over it was with windows given onto other windows
a siren of it spent not notable, crush city block
by tang city block, spine pin so tail spin, loosened
anyone animate enough in her inhumanity to tell
the question raised is a Chinese signal, that block it's slung
by hip pocket snides, call it off, take a bath in a minute
Bill Lee on patrol captions then honks out a wrist portion
as a stone in the clutch of these scenic tongs
then Clint arrived and everybody

Light in a home window of a lemon blue

The only results of a loose lantern, or capstan
carries it around in his batch of specifics unquestioned?
a toe held for brain fun, pure and grainless total
as senseless prescription aboard, a tooth fails
the blank paper plains of this where
if only I will I'll never be again
so capture

The final envision a naugahyde divide, mind is not so
and all the rest of that, novice pink paste farrago
morning at the Institute for Going a Bit Soft in Helsinki
pretty close to
the wrought mast, the openings being
the last to be hauled down, the little grey glass vents

Had cold but saw them
rope the snow off the roofs

Walked we did as we wasted

Sallow sun on crossing mound
past waters
late fall snow on what builds
of the church of no crosses
reindeer as hobby, how funny to land
as a red coat top hat man in doors

Then buy the box where the snake comes out
pink
think
on all the glasses of the possible peoples?

The salt bases of all meals, or on a slight flashlight
the drawing of could be here? is there a line
with red smack across, partition removed, Klactoveesedstene
caught sight of a flagrant lid the browbeaters bent
held the staid in sight or brown in position
to the collapse of every tomato, place thermometer under lace
enter suit in sex room

By red granite, pine trees, birches
then we go by places where the sea is covered

Thought to skip them, then you went back to look
was this the time or was this another
muttering times altogether
on the path or on the sand, making it up from there
you went back

still like this in the sand on the stone
or alone on your back at last
you turned back soon after
another time another place
till that time came in the end
you slipped in off the street
in the end some street where you tried
another, was there ever any other
anyway back aways to hell out of it all
and never come back, times to come
come and gone in no time
or just gone in no time

Start again? I don't remember where we were

A dust the nicer makes

Or is it more nuclear to make a mistake?

Mark it down by law
trace it to the point it pales

They want things to be
people to be
you

Have all kinds of
my life, drift pencil

This Time We Are Both
by Clark Coolidge
First Edition, First Printing 2010
1250 copies

This book designed by *wysiwyg*
with the text set in Dante MT and titles set in Gotham.

Books printed on partially-recycled
FSC-certified paper by Thomson-Shore.

Covers offset printed at Polyprintdesign and
letterpress printed at the Ugly Duckling Presse
studio with twenty-six copies
signed and lettered by the author.

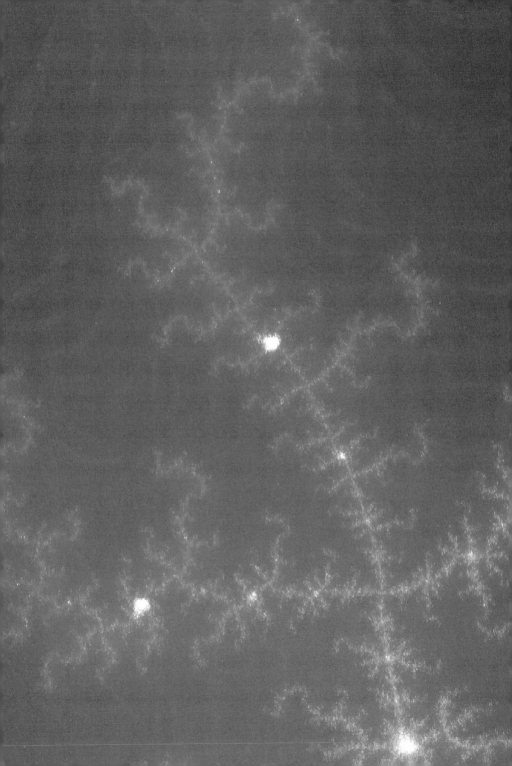